Arranged for all portable keyboards *by Kenneth Baker.*

THE COMPLETE KEYBOARD PLAYER

BOOK 3

About This Book **3**

LESSONS

1 Chord of E7 4

2 Chord of E Minor Em 8

3 Scale of C; Key of C; Scale of F;
   Key of F 12
   Chord of B♭; Chord of F7 13

4 Triplets; Sixteenth notes (semiquavers),
   and dotted rhythms 20

5 Scale of G; Key of G; Chord of B7 24

6 Chords of G Minor Gm,
   and B♭ Minor B♭m 28

7 Minor keys; Key of D Minor 32

8 Key of E Minor 36

9 Key of B Flat; Chord of E♭ (Major) 40

10 Chord of C Minor Cm 44
    Chord Chart 48

SONGS

A Woman In Love 38

Bright Eyes 8

Callan (Sogno Nostalgico) 37

Chanson D'Amour 24

Don't Cry For Me Argentina 41

(Everything I Do) I Do It For You 30

Falling 16

Hava Nagila 34

I Left My Heart In San Francisco 6

Isn't She Lovely 29

Mamma Mia 42

Ob La Di, Ob La Da 14

Raindrops Keep Falling On My Head 44

Star Wars (Main Theme) 46

Sunny 33

(They Long To Be) Close To You 22

Tulips From Amsterdam 18

When I'm Sixty Four 26

Where Is Your Heart
(The Song From Moulin Rouge) 10

Winner Takes It All (The) 4

Wise Publications
London/New York/Paris/Sydney/Copenhagen/Madrid

Exclusive Distributors:
Music Sales Limited
8/9 Frith Street, London W1V 5TZ, England.

Music Sales Pty Limited
120 Rothschild Avenue, Rosebery, NSW 2018, Australia.

This book © Copyright 1994 by
Wise Publications
Order No. AM91385
ISBN 0-7119-3650-1

Your Guarantee of Quality
As publishers, we strive to produce every book to the
highest commercial standards.
Particular care has been given to specifying acid-free, neutral-sized paper
made from pulps which have not been elemental chlorine bleached.
This pulp is from farmed sustainable forests and was produced with
special regard for the environment.
Throughout, the printing and binding have been planned to ensure a sturdy,
attractive publication which should give years of enjoyment.
If your copy fails to meet our high standards, please inform
us and we will gladly replace it.

Music Sales' complete catalogue describes thousands of titles and is
available in full colour sections by subject, direct from Music Sales Limited.
Please state your areas of interest and send a cheque/postal order for £1.50 for postage to:
Music Sales Limited, Newmarket Road, Bury St. Edmunds,
Suffolk IP33 3YB.

Printed in the United Kingdom by
Halstan & Co Limited, Amersham, Buckinghamshire.

ABOUT THIS BOOK

In Book 3 of *The Complete Keyboard Player* you learn about scales and keys. When you play in different keys you make basic changes of sound, and so add a new dimension to your playing. Minor keys, especially, can change the whole flavour of your music. In Book 3 you play in five new keys, including two minor keys.

In Book 3 you continue your left hand studies, with the emphasis as usual on 'fingered' chords. Nine new chords are introduced, in easy stages, and all the chords used in the series appear in the Chord Chart at the back of the book.

There is plenty for your right hand in Book 3. There are double notes, chords, fill-ins and counter-melodies.

As usual, throughout the book you will get tips on how to use the facilities of the keyboard–the sounds, the rhythms, and so on–more effectively.

Although Book 3 continues in the 'teach yourself' tradition of the earlier books, all teachers of the instrument will want to make it one of their standard text books.

The optional matching CD or cassette, on which you can hear the author playing all the songs from the book, will help you to learn even faster!

1 CHORD OF E♭7

Using single-finger chord method:

Locate "E♭" (the higher one of two) in the accompaniment section of your keyboard.
Convert this note into E♭7 (see Book One, page 42ff., and your owner's manual).

Using fingered chord method:

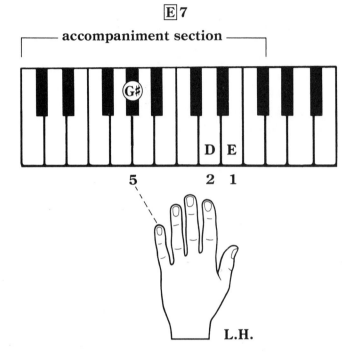

THE WINNER TAKES IT ALL

Words & Music by Benny Andersson & Bjorn Ulvaeus

Suggested registration: piano

Rhythm: rock
Tempo: medium (♩ = 112)
Synchro-start: on

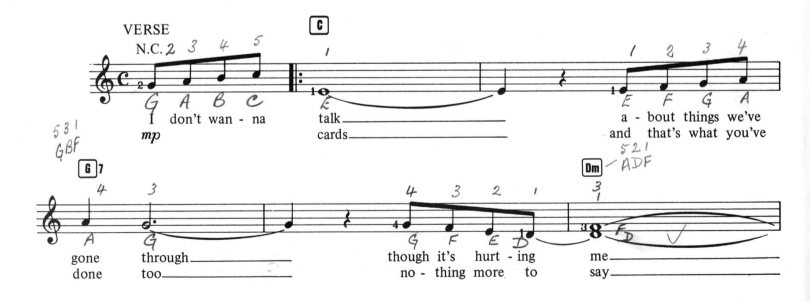

I LEFT MY HEART IN SAN FRANCISCO

Words by Douglas Cross
Music by George Cory

Suggested registration: string ensemble

Rhythm: swing
Tempo: fairly slow (♩ = 96)
Synchro-start: on

CHORD OF E MINOR Em

Using single-finger chord method:

Locate "E" (the higher one of two) in the accompaniment section of your keyboard. Convert this note into Em (see Book Two, page 28, and your owner's manual).

Using fingered chord method:

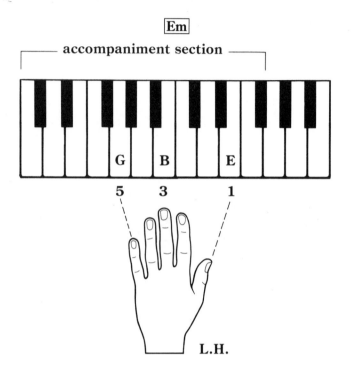

BRIGHT EYES

Words & Music by Mike Batt

Suggested registration: electric guitar + arpeggio

Rhythm: rock
Tempo: medium (♩ = 96)
Synchro-start: on

9

THE SONG FROM "MOULIN ROUGE"
(WHERE IS YOUR HEART?)

Words by William Engvick
Music by Georges Auric

Suggested registration: hawaiian guitar

Rhythm: waltz
Tempo: slow (♩ = 88)
Synchro-start: on

*Split these two notes (playing lower note first).

3 SCALE OF C; KEY OF C

A scale is a succession of adjoining notes:

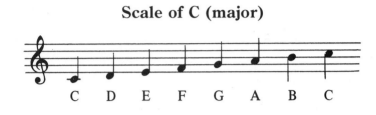

Scale of C (major)

As you see, there are no black notes in the scale of C.

When a piece is built on this scale it is said to be in the "key of C".
Almost all the pieces you have played so far have been in the key of C.
The occasional black notes you encountered in those pieces were of
a temporary nature only, and did not affect the overall key.

From now on you are going to play in a number of different keys for the sake
of contrast.

SCALE OF F; KEY OF F

Scale of F (major)

As you see, a B Flat is required to form the scale of F. When you are playing in
this key, therefore, you must remember to play all your B's, wherever they might
fall on the keyboard, as B Flats.

To remind you, a B Flat is inserted at the beginning of every line:-

key signature

To help you further, I have arrowed the first few B Flats in the following songs.

CHORD OF Bb ; CHORD OF F7

You need these two chords in order to play in the Key of F.

Using single-finger chord method:

Locate "Bb" in the accompaniment section of your keyboard. Play this note on its own and you will have a chord of Bb (major).

Locate "F" (the lower one of two) in the accompaniment section of your keyboard. Convert this into F7 (see Book One, page 42ff., and your owner's manual).

Using fingered chord method:

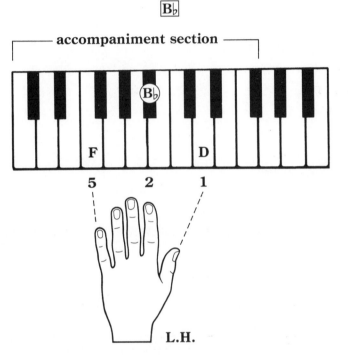

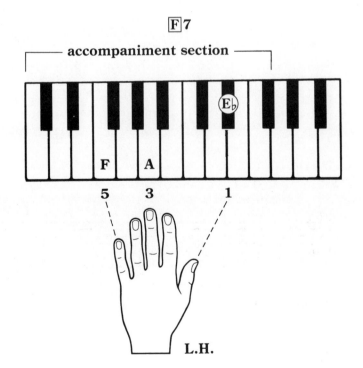

OB-LA-DI, OB-LA-DA

Words & Music by John Lennon & Paul McCartney

Suggested registration: funny

Rhythm: swing
Tempo: fast (♩ = 112)
Synchro-start: on

*Cut Common Time. A feeling of two in a bar (²₂) rather than four (⁴₄).
Notice the metronome marking: ♩ = 112.

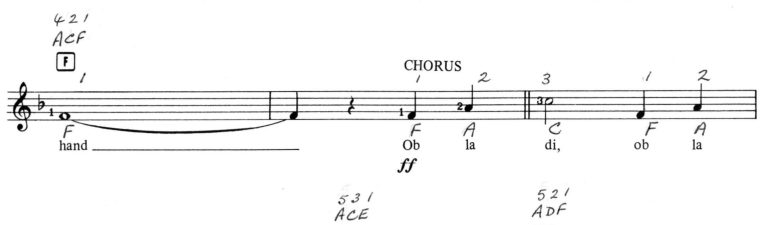

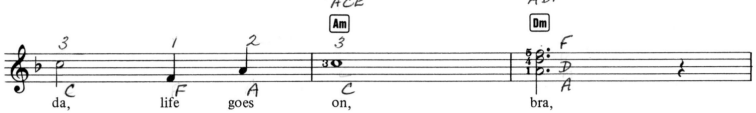

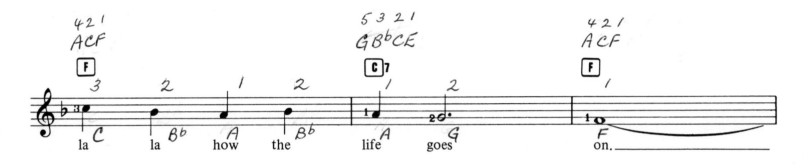

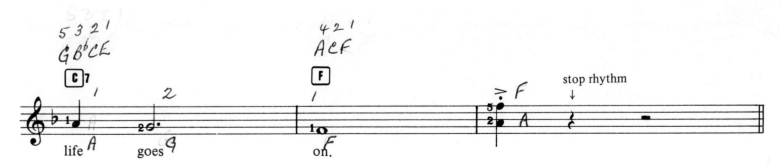

FALLING

Words & Music by Angelo Badalamenti & David Lynch

Suggested registration: guitar

Rhythm: rock
Tempo: slow (♩ = 100)
Synchro-start: on

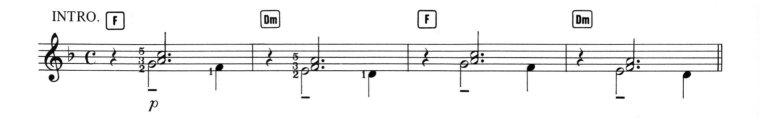

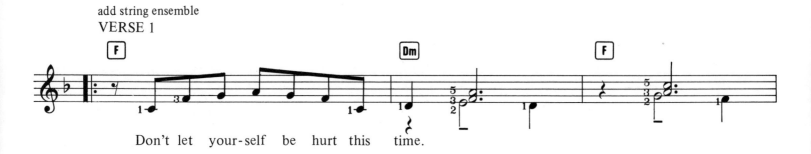

add string ensemble
VERSE 1

Don't let your-self be hurt this time.

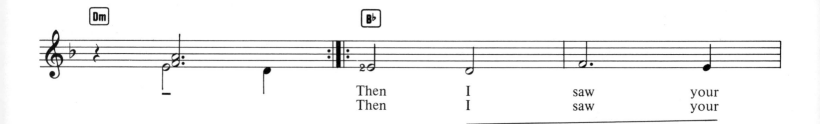

Then   I   saw   your
Then   I   saw   your

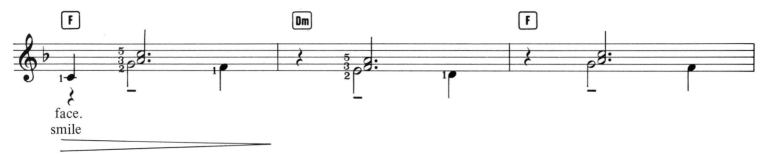

face.
smile

VERSE 2

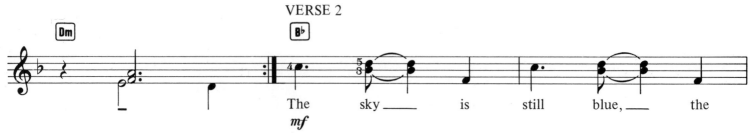

The   sky ___   is   still   blue, ___   the

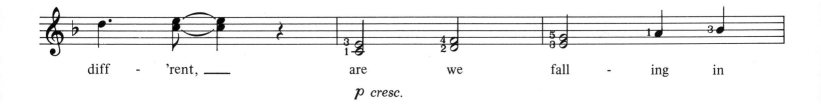
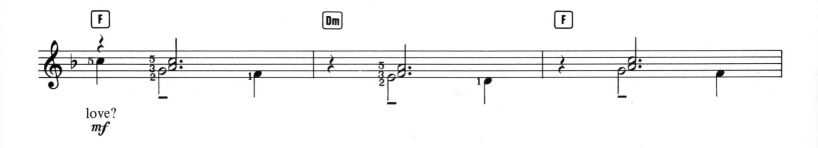

TULIPS FROM AMSTERDAM

English Words by Gene Martyn
Original Words by Neumann and Bader
Music by Ralf Arnie

Suggested registration: accordion

Rhythm: waltz
Tempo: fast (= 184)
Synchro-start: on

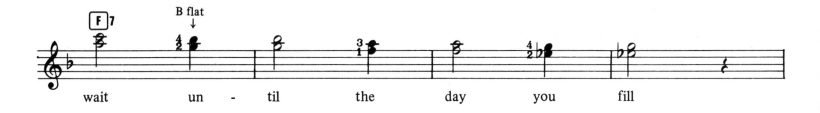

wait un - til the day you fill

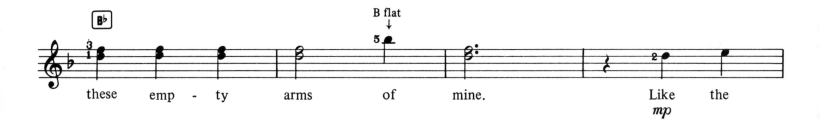

these emp - ty arms of mine. Like the
mp

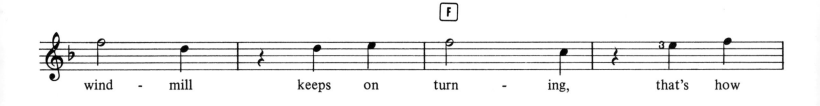

wind - mill keeps on turn - ing, that's how

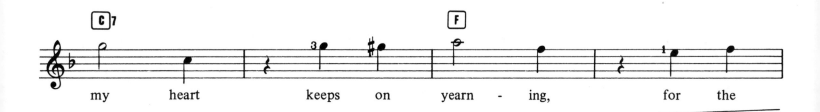

my heart keeps on yearn - ing, for the

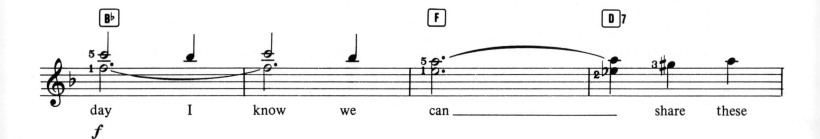

day I know we can _____ share these
f

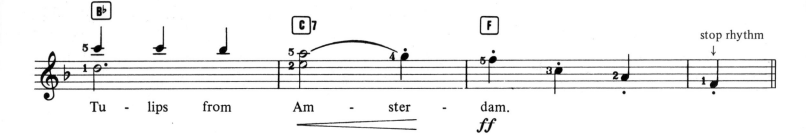

Tu - lips from Am - ster - dam.
ff

4 TRIPLETS

A triplet is a group of 3 notes played in the time of 2:-

Eighth Note (Quaver) Triplets must be played slightly FASTER than normal eighth notes, in order to fit them to the beat. Compare the following two examples:-

ex. 1   normal eighth notes (quavers)

ex. 2   eighth note (quaver) triplets

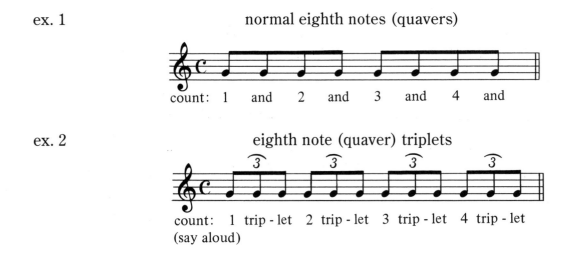

If you incorporate the word "triplet" into your counting like this, you will get the feeling of the triplets.

SIXTEENTH NOTES (SEMIQUAVERS), AND DOTTED RHYTHMS

An eighth note (quaver) can be subdivided into two sixteenth notes (semiquavers):-

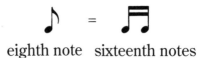

eighth note   sixteenth notes

A "dotted" eighth note is equal to half as much again (see "dotted time notes", Book Two, page 29), that is, three sixteenth notes:-

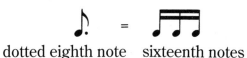

dotted eighth note   sixteenth notes

In practice, a dotted eighth note usually pairs up with a sixteenth note:-

dotted eighth note sixteenth note

Together these two time notes are equivalent to 4 sixteenth notes, or 1 quarter note (crotchet):-

3 sixteenth notes + 1 sixteenth note = quarter note

The general effect of a passage like:-

is of eighth notes (quavers) with a "lilt". The phrase "humpty dumpty" can be used as a guide to this rhythm:-

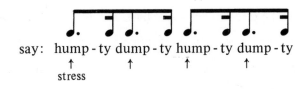

say: hump - ty dump - ty hump - ty dump - ty

stress

These uneven types of rhythms are often called "Dotted Rhythms". Look out for dotted rhythms in the next four pieces.

In *Close To You*, watch out for "normal" eighth notes, eighth note triplets, and dotted rhythms.

(THEY LONG TO BE) CLOSE TO YOU

Words by Hal David. Music by Burt Bacharach

Suggested registration: piano

Rhythm: swing
Tempo: medium ($\downarrow$ = 96)
Synchro-start: on

*A **CODA** is a section, usually quite short, added to a piece of music to make an ending.
DAL SEGNO AL CODA (*D.S. al CODA*) means go back to the sign: 𝄋 and play through the same music again, until: "*to CODA* ⊕". From here jump to *CODA* and play through to the end.

5 SCALE OF G; KEY OF G

Scale of G (major)

G A B C D E (F♯) G

An F Sharp is required to form the scale of G. When a piece is built on this scale it is said to be in the "key of G". When you are playing in this key you must remember to play all Fs, wherever they might fall on the keyboard, as F Sharps. The key signature, which appears at the beginning of every line, will remind you:-

key signature   Key of G

CHORD OF B7

Using single-finger chord method:

Locate "B" in the accompaniment section of your keyboard. Convert this into B7 (see Book One, page 42ff., and your owner's manual).

Using fingered chord method:

CHANSON D'AMOUR

Words & Music by Wayne Shanklin

Suggested registration: choir

Rhythm: swing
Tempo: medium (♩ = 100)
Synchro-start: on

G   A7   Am

p Chan - son d'a - mour _____
Chan - son d'a - mour _____

F sharp   D7   F sharp

ra da da da da,   play en - core_
ra da da da da,   je t'a - dore_

mf

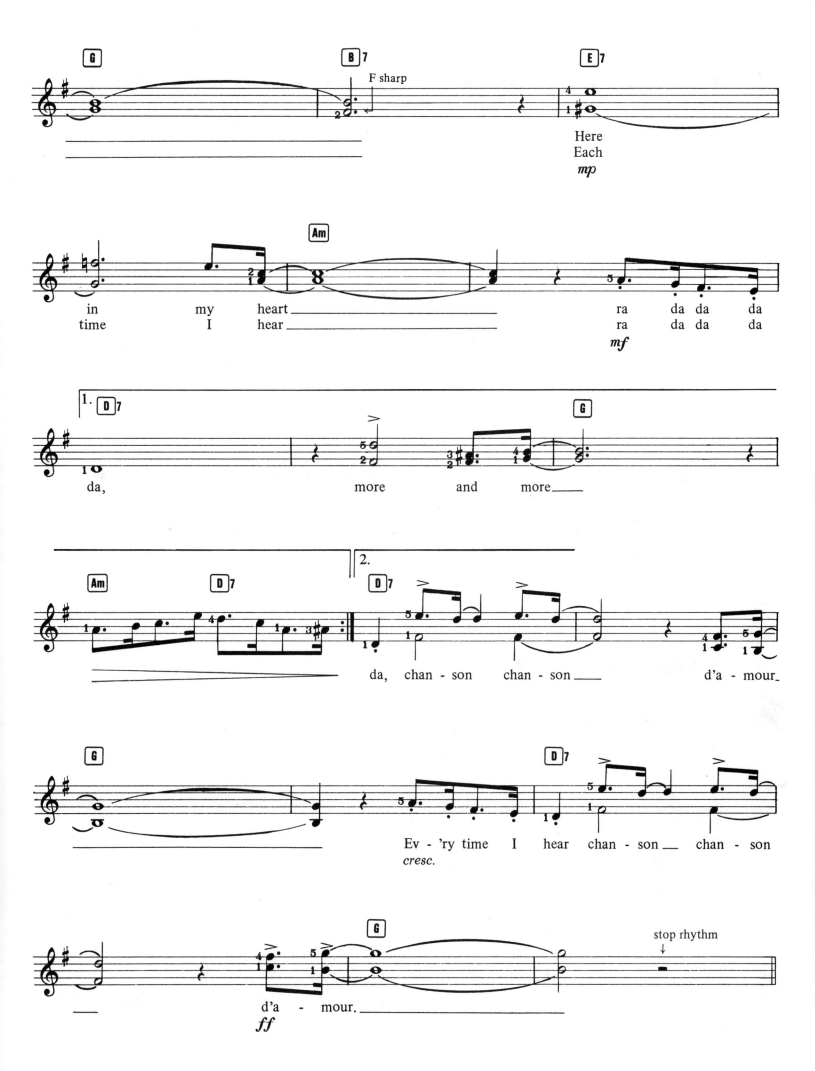

WHEN I'M SIXTY-FOUR

Words & Music by John Lennon & Paul McCartney

Suggested registration: clarinet

Rhythm: swing
Tempo: medium (♩ = 112)
Synchro-start: on

*Leave synchro button on, and rhythm will start again automatically when you strike the next chord ("G", at the beginning of the piece).

6 CHORDS OF G MINOR Gm , AND B♭ MINOR B♭m

Using single-finger chord method:

Locate "G" and "B♭" in the accompaniment section of your keyboard. Convert these notes into Gm and B♭m respectively (see Book Two, page 28, and your owner's manual).

Using fingered chord method:

Gm

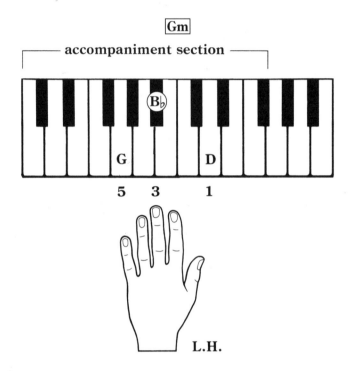

Compare this chord with G (major), a chord you already know.

B♭m

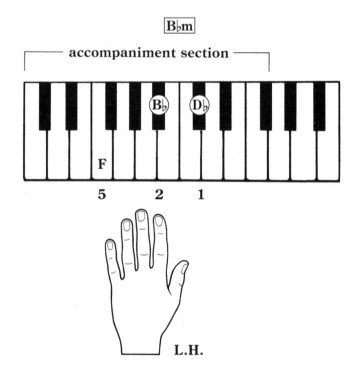

Compare this chord with B♭ (major), a chord you already know.

ISN'T SHE LOVELY

Words & Music by Stevie Wonder

Suggested registration: piano + sustain

Rhythm: swing
Tempo: medium (♩ = 112)
Synchro-start: on

*QUARTER NOTE (CROTCHET) TRIPLET. 3 quarter notes played in the time of 2. Play these quarter notes slightly faster than usual, in order to fit them into the bar, but keep them even, and equal to each other.

(EVERYTHING I DO) I DO IT FOR YOU

Words & Music by Bryan Adams, R.J. Lange and M. Kamen

Suggested registration: flute

Rhythm: 8 beat
Tempo: slow (♩ = 80)
Synchro-start: on

7 | MINOR KEYS

So far almost all your playing has been in major keys: C, F, and G. Songs written in minor keys, with their preponderance of minor chords, often have a sad, nostalgic quality, which makes an excellent contrast.

KEY OF D MINOR

The key of D Minor is related to the key of F Major. The scales on which these keys are built use the same notes:

Scale of D Minor ('natural')

D   E   F   G   A   (B♭)   C   D

Scale of F

F   G   A   (B♭)   C   D   E   F

All the notes are white except one: B Flat. As you would expect, both keys have the same key signature:

Key of D Minor

Key of F

When playing in the key of D Minor (as in the key of F), you must remember to play all B's, wherever they might fall on the keyboard, as B Flats.

SUNNY

Words & Music by Bobby Hebb

Suggested registration: *jazz organ, with stereo chorus.*

Rhythm: rock
Tempo: medium (♩ = 96)
Synchro-start: on

Sun - ny
mp
yes - ter - day my life was filled with

rain. Sun - ny
you smiled at me and

real - ly eased the pain, oh the dark days are done and the
cresc.

bright days are here, my Sun - ny one shines so sin - cere, oh, Sun - ny one so
mf

true, I love you.
f
f

HAVA NAGILA

Traditional

Suggested registration: bass clarinet

Rhythm: march $\frac{2}{4}$ (or swing)

Tempo: medium ($\quarternote$ = 112)

(Speed up tempo control, bit by bit, with left hand)

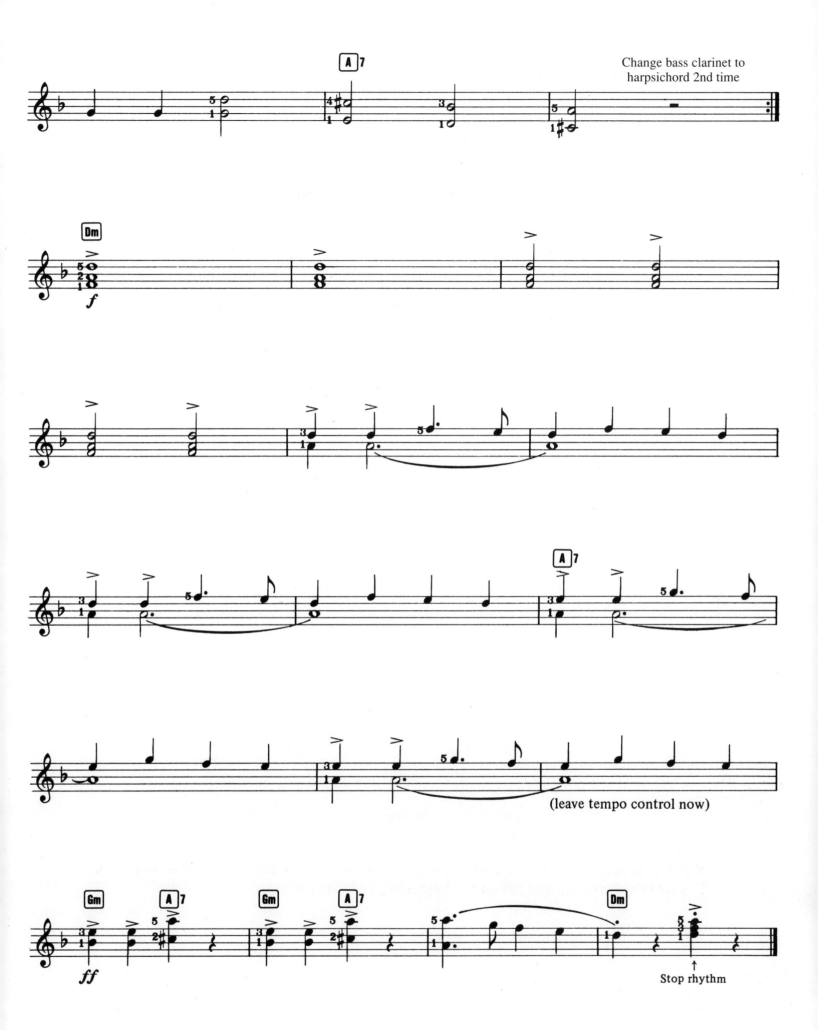

KEY OF E MINOR

The key of E Minor is related to the key of G Major. Both keys use the same scale notes:

Scale of E Minor ('natural')

E F♯ G A B C D E

Scale of G

G A B C D E F♯ G

All the notes are white except one: F Sharp.

The key signature is the same for both keys:

Key of E Minor

Key of G

When playing in the key of E Minor (as in the key of G), you must remember to play all F's, wherever they might fall on the keyboard, as F Sharps.

CALLAN (SOGNO NOSTALGICO)

By Armando Sciascia

Suggested registration: guitar

Rhythm: waltz
Tempo: slow (♩ = 88)
Synchro-start: on

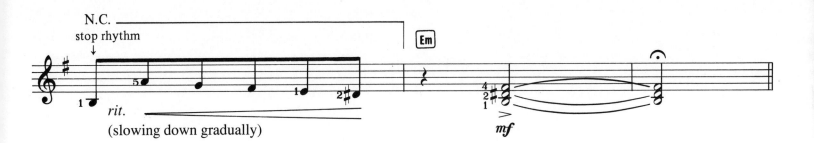

A WOMAN IN LOVE

Words & Music by Barry Gibb & Robin Gibb

Suggested registration: flute

Rhythm: 8 beat
Tempo: medium (♩ = 96)
Synchro-start: on

9 KEY OF B FLAT

The scale of B Flat, and therefore the key of B Flat, requires two flats: B Flat, and E Flat:-

Scale / Key of B Flat (major)

When you are playing in this key you must remember to play all B's and E's, wherever they might fall on the keyboard, as B Flats and E Flats, respectively.

CHORD OF E♭ (MAJOR)

Using single-finger chord method:

Play the note "E♭" (the higher one of two) in the accompaniment section of your keyboard.

Using fingered chord method:

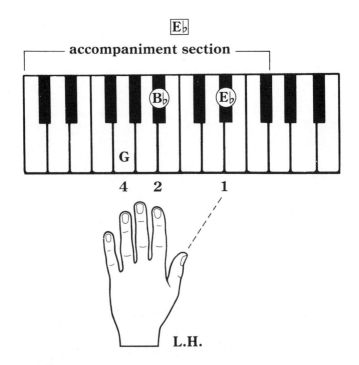

DON'T CRY FOR ME ARGENTINA

Music by Andrew Lloyd Webber
Lyrics by Tim Rice

Suggested registration: trumpet

Rhythm: tango
Tempo: medium (♩ = 112)
Synchro-start: on

MAMMA MIA

Words & Music by Benny Andersson, Stig Anderson
& Bjorn Alvaeus

Suggested registration: oboe

Rhythm: rock
Tempo: medium (♩ = 126)
Synchro-start: on

I've been cheat-ed by you___ since I don't know when.
So I made up my mind___ it must come to an end.

Look at me now___ will I ev - er learn?

I don't know how___ but I sud - den - ly lose___ con - trol

There's a fire ___ with - in my soul _____ just a

look and I can hear a bell ring ___ One more look and I for - get ev - 'ry - thing___

CHORUS

Oh _____ Mam-ma Mi - a! Here I go _____ a - gain,

my, my! How can I re - sist you? Mam-ma Mi - a!

Does it show _____ a - gain, my, my! Just how much I've missed you.

Yes _____ I've been bro - ken heart - ed, blue _____ since the day _____

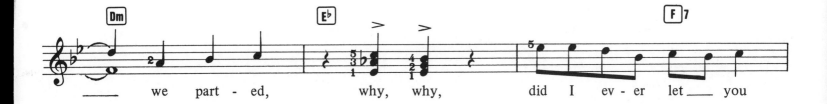

_____ we part - ed, why, why, did I ev - er let _____ you

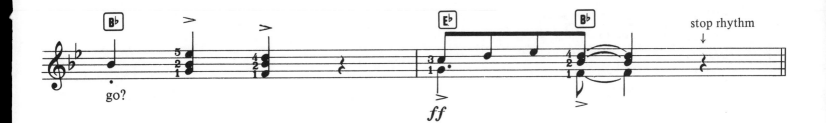

go?

ff

stop rhythm

CHORD OF C MINOR [Cm]

Using single-finger chord method:

Locate "C" (the higher one of two) in the accompaniment section of your keyboard.
Convert this note into [Cm] (see Book Two, page 28, and your owner's manual).

Using fingered chord method:

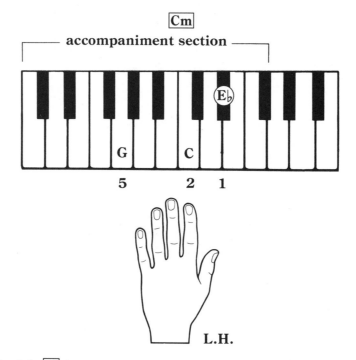

Compare this chord with [C] (major), a chord you already know.

RAINDROPS KEEP FALLING ON MY HEAD

Words by Hal David
Music by Burt Bacharach

Suggested registration: whistle

Rhythm: swing
Tempo: medium (♩ = 104)
Synchro-start: on

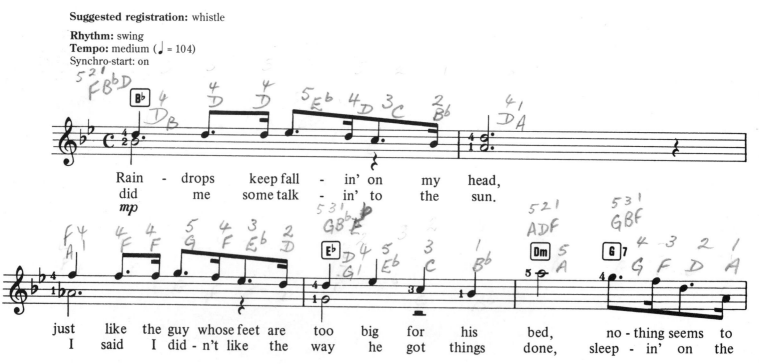

Rain - drops   keep fall - in' on   my   head,
did   me   some talk - in' to   the   sun.

just   like the guy whose feet are   too   big   for   his   bed,   no - thing seems to
I   said   I did - n't like the   way   he   got   things done,   sleep - in' on the

fit, those rain - drops are fall - in' on my head, they keep fall - in', ___
job, those rain - drops are fall - in' on my head, they keep fall - in', ___

whistle to vibes 2nd time

So I just
But there's one thing I know, the

blues they send to meet me won't de - feat me, it

cresc.

won't be long ___ till hap - pi - ness steps up to greet ___ me.

D.C. al Coda

⊕ *CODA*

Be - cause I'm

free ___ no-thin's wor-ry-ing me. ___

stop rhythm

*DA CAPO AL CODA (*D.C. al Coda*) means go back to the beginning of the piece and play through the same music again, until: "*to CODA* ⊕". From here jump to *CODA* and play through to the end.

STAR WARS (THEME)

By John Williams

Suggested registration: brass ensemble

Rhythm: disco
Tempo: medium (♩ = 112)
Synchro-start: on

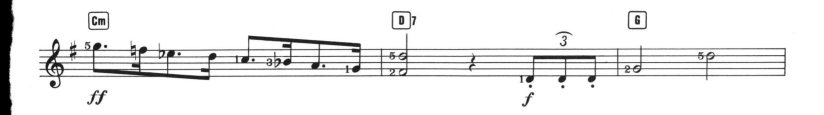

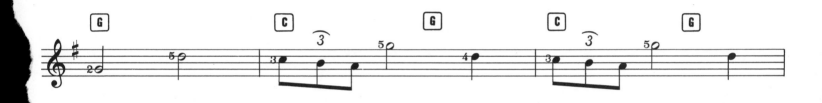

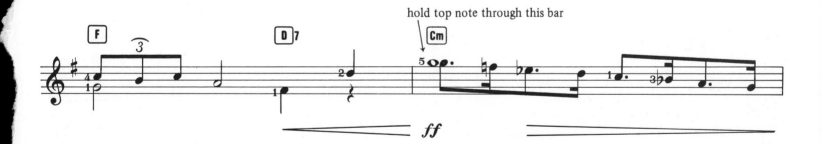

hold top note through this bar

stop rhythm

CHORD CHART (Showing all "fingered chords" used in the course so far)

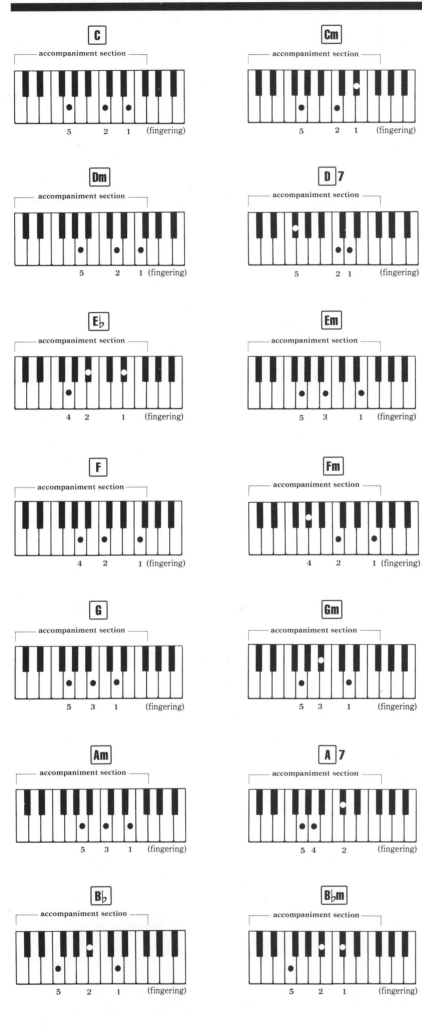

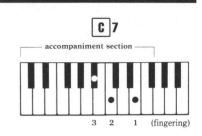

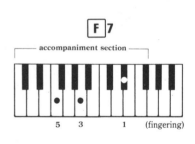

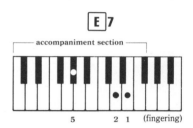

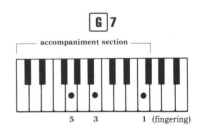

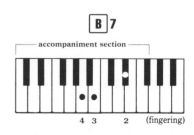

1/98 (29727)